THE WIRE ZOO

How Elizabeth Berrien Learned to Turn Wire into Amazing Art

Written by **NATASHA WING** and illustrated by **JOANIE STONE**

A Paula Wiseman Book
Simon & Schuster Books for Young Readers
New York   London   Toronto   Sydney   New Delhi

SIMON & SCHUSTER BOOKS FOR YOUNG READERS An imprint of Simon & Schuster Children's Publishing Division | 1230 Avenue of the Americas, New York, New York 10020 | Text © 2024 by Natasha Wing | Illustration © 2024 by Joanie Stone | Photography © 2024 by Elizabeth Berrien | Book design by Sarah Creech | All rights reserved, including the right of reproduction in whole or in part in any form. SIMON & SCHUSTER BOOKS FOR YOUNG READERS and related marks are trademarks of Simon & Schuster, LLC. Simon & Schuster: Celebrating 100 Years of Publishing in 2024 | For information about special discounts for bulk purchases, please contact Simon & Schuster Special Sales at 1-866-506-1949 or business@simonandschuster.com. | The Simon & Schuster Speakers Bureau can bring authors to your live event. For more information or to book an event, contact the Simon & Schuster Speakers Bureau at 1-866-248-3049 or visit our website at www.simonspeakers.com. | The text for this book was set in New Caledonia. | The illustrations for this book were rendered digitally using Procreate and Photoshop. Manufactured in China | 0624 SCP | First Edition

2 4 6 8 10 9 7 5 3 1

Library of Congress Cataloging-in-Publication Data | Names: Wing, Natasha, author. | Stone, Joanie, illustrator. Title: The wire zoo : the story of wire sculptor Elizabeth Berrien / Natasha Wing ; illustrated by Joanie Stone. Description: First edition. | New York, New York : Simon & Schuster Books for Young Readers, [2024] | Includes bibliographical references. | Audience: Ages 4–8 | Audience: Grades 2–3 | Summary: "This inspirational picture book biography tells the story of how neurodivergent artist Elizabeth Berrien created three-dimensional wire sculptures and went on to become a leader of the contemporary wire sculpture movement"— Provided by publisher. Identifiers: LCCN 2023050791 (print) | LCCN 2023050792 (ebook) | ISBN 9781665940764 (hardcover) | ISBN 9781665940771 (ebook) | Subjects: LCSH: Berrien, Elizabeth (Wire sculptor—Juvenile literature. | Sculptors—United States—Biography—Juvenile literature. | Women sculptors—United States—Biography—Juvenile literature. | Wire in art. Classification: LCC NB237.B4385 W56 2024 (print) | LCC NB237.B4385 (ebook) | DDC 730.92—dc23/eng/20231205 LC record available at https://lccn.loc.gov/2023050791

LC ebook record available at https://lccn.loc.gov/2023050792

To artist extraordinaire, Elizabeth Berrien, thank you for your patience and input all those years while developing this story. And to children with minds that see in unique ways—you are our future inventors!
—N. W.

To all the art teachers—thank you
—J. S.

Elizabeth Berrien has always loved animals. She wished she could surround herself with them for the rest of her life. There were always pets in the house— dogs, cats, fish, and a ferret. Her first pet was a turtle.

But Elizabeth saw animals in a special way. Her mind imagined lines flowing across the surface of their bodies. Thin lines and thick lines. Bright lines and dim lines.

She traveled along on a magical ride inside the lines, following the swoop of an elephant's trunk . . . the zigzag of hair in a cat's ear . . . the spiral of a snail's shell. To Elizabeth the flowing lines made each animal unique and beautiful. She wondered, *How can I copy these lines so others can see them too?*

Elizabeth decided to draw them. She'd never been very good at drawing. But she wanted to try.

Her sister Zan put a crayon in Elizabeth's right hand. "Hold it like this," she said, curling Elizabeth's little fingers around the crayon.

But instead of creating swooping, smooth lines, Elizabeth's hand just made scribbles that went all over the place.

"Don't worry," said Zan. "You'll figure it out when you're older."

Elizabeth kept trying. But nothing she drew looked like the beautiful lines she saw. If only her mind and hand could work together.

One day while daydreaming, Elizabeth gazed up at the cracks in the ceiling. A long imaginary line appeared! She pictured the line looping around a crack, again and again. There had to be a way to recreate what she was seeing!

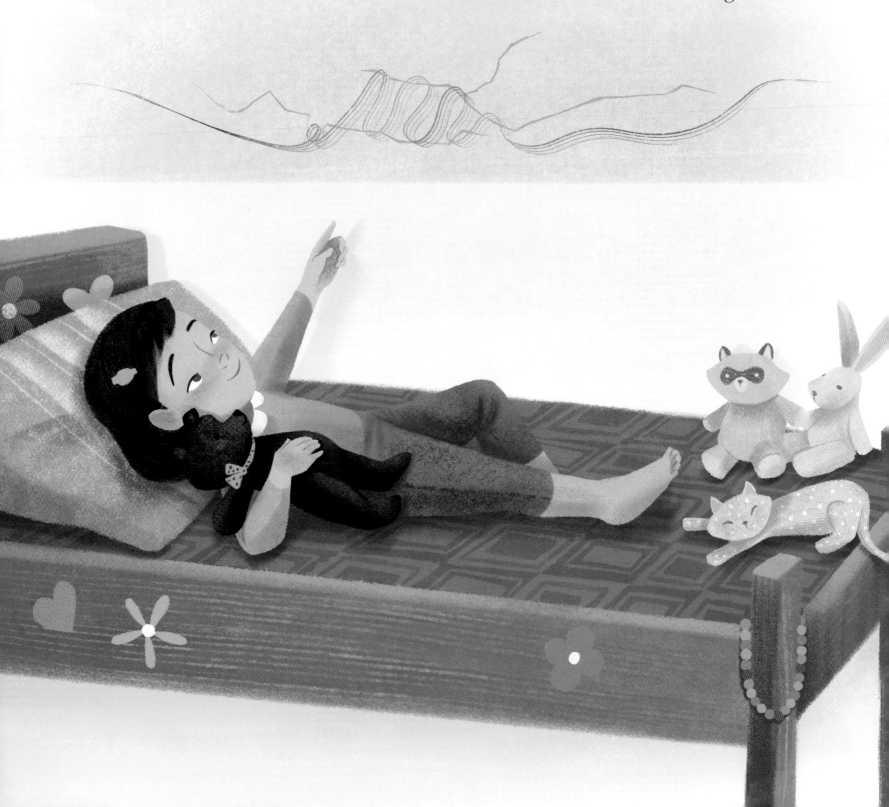

She spotted a pencil and a piece of string on her dresser. She wrapped the string around and around the pencil. It still didn't look right. Then Elizabeth got an idea.

She found a second pencil. Using the two pencils like knitting needles, she looped and hooked the string into one row, then two, then three—until at last she had made a square. A lumpy, knotted square.

It was the most wonderful thing she'd ever made with her own two hands. And it was the closest she'd ever gotten to recreating the lines she saw.

As she got older, Elizabeth learned how to knit scarves with yarn, make delicate lace, weave mats with palm fronds, and form tiny baskets with pine needles. When she had to use her weaker right hand, her brain began rewiring her eyes and hands to work together. Elizabeth found that using two hands to make things was much easier than one.

Spending hours crafting made Elizabeth as happy as a bee in a field of wildflowers. But she still couldn't figure out how to recreate the flowing lines she saw on animals. If only she could make something to show people how beautiful the lines were.

In high school Elizabeth signed up for an art class. She hoped to finally learn how to draw better. Elizabeth had still never figured out how to draw "good" lines. She had always been taught to use her right hand, even though she was left-handed. Her art teacher was strict though. She wanted her students to draw straight, perfect lines. No scribbles or smudges were allowed.

The teacher scolded Elizabeth in front of the class for her sloppy work.
Elizabeth rebelled by drawing the ugliest, messiest portrait she could.
Art should make me feel happy, thought Elizabeth. *Then why do I feel so sad?*
Elizabeth finally gave up and swore she'd never take another art class again until . . .

The school placed her in a new, experimental sculpture class. Elizabeth threatened to walk out. She was done with art! Luckily, the teacher, Mr. Curran, was kind and open-minded. He convinced her to stay.

"You'll have more fun with art if you think of things in terms of creative problem-solving," he said.

Elizabeth took his advice to heart. She realized she wouldn't be able to do art her way unless she understood the different forms. So she learned *all* the equipment—from kilns to looms to propane torches. With each new medium she tried, more of her joy returned. Art became fun again!

Still, nothing she created looked like the lines she saw.

But everything changed the day Mr. Curran gave her a roll of wire.

The wire was thin and smooth between her fingers. Elizabeth cut a long strand. With both hands, she pulled and curved then crimped and pinched. A bend became an ear. A twist, a whisker. Her mind, eyes, hands, and the wire worked together to create a cat!

Finally she'd found the thing that expressed the beauty she'd seen all her life.

Discovering wire art lit a spark in Elizabeth. Day and night, she bent and snipped, tweaked and squeezed. If a line didn't look right, she simply bent it around until it did. But Elizabeth had a new problem to solve: How would she hold the wire together so her animals could be 3D, like in real life?

In school Mr. Curran helped her use a propane torch to melt a piece of metal called solder onto where the wires crossed. When the solder hardened, it joined the wires together, making the connection stronger. But at home, her parents forbade her from using a torch, so she had to figure out another way to join the wire without using heat.

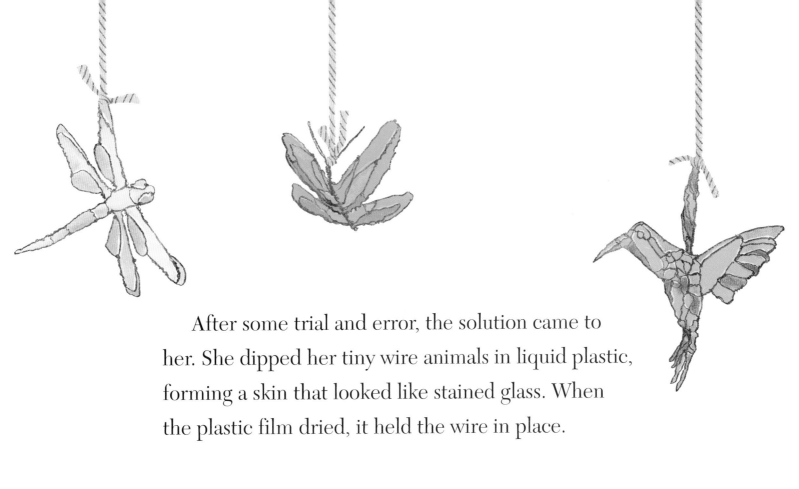

After some trial and error, the solution came to her. She dipped her tiny wire animals in liquid plastic, forming a skin that looked like stained glass. When the plastic film dried, it held the wire in place.

After high school Elizabeth tried selling her coated, hand-twisted wire animals at craft fairs. Every time someone stopped by her booth and picked up an animal, Elizabeth perked up. *Will they like it enough to buy it?*

She watched them turn the piece around in their hands, her heart beating faster. When they put it back down on the table, she couldn't help feeling a little disappointed. But she didn't let it get to her—she still thanked them for taking the time to look at her art. She was determined to keep practicing, and hopefully as her animals got better, someone would finally buy one.

Then at one fair someone exclaimed, "Look at that wire inside!" The other customers noticed too and asked if Elizabeth could make her animals without the coating. It was the plain wire they wanted to see.

Without the coating Elizabeth knew the animals wouldn't be strong enough to stand. And soldering wouldn't work with this kind of wire. But she found joy in this new problem and was determined to solve it. She told the people that she'd give it a try.

At home she started working the wire with her hands, the way she had with the string and pencils so many years ago, over and under. She then intertwined it like basket weaving and looped it like lace. She followed the map of lines in her mind.

When at last she set her little deer down, it stood!

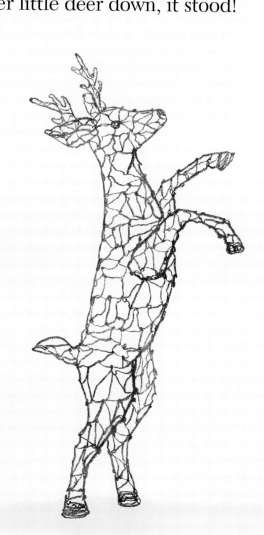

At the next fair, she displayed her bare wire animals. What would people think of her animals now that they weren't bright and colorful? Elizabeth held her breath as a customer picked up and inspected a tiny leaping deer. "I'd like to buy this," she said at last. Elizabeth let out a breath. If the lines on *her* surface were visible, they'd be glowing.

As Elizabeth took her money, the customer added,
"You are a true wire sculptor."

Wire sculptor. Elizabeth liked the sound of that.

Buzzing with energy and ideas,
Elizabeth explored what else she
could do with wire.

She played with florist wire. Beading wire. Aluminum and copper wire. She mixed wire of different colors, sizes, and materials. She gave up using pliers.

She wanted everything to come from her mind directly to her hands. Her sore fingers became scratched, blistered, and callused. But as they grew tougher, her skills got better and her sculptures more detailed.

A friend's cousin worked at a big department store in San Francisco. His team was searching for new ideas for their Christmas windows. He thought of Elizabeth and invited her to one of their meetings. Elizabeth brought a box of her tiny wire animals and a life-sized horse head she'd just created.

When everyone saw the horse head they exclaimed, "We want three horses—with wings—for the Christmas windows!"

Elizabeth could hardly believe the request. *Can I actually do this?* she wondered. Up until then, she had only made small pieces. She had never attempted a complete life-sized animal sculpture, let alone three horses with wings! Still, it was too big of an opportunity to pass up. She agreed to make the sculptures for the Christmas windows.

Back at home Elizabeth found joy in solving this new problem of how to create life-sized sculptures. She suspended the wire horse head from cabin rafters and worked from the head down, twisting and crimping until her fingers were sore. She pushed through the pain. She pushed through her fear of failure. She pushed through early mornings and late nights until all three of the flying horses were done.

On the night before Thanksgiving, Elizabeth helped the crew install her three flying horses. They had been painted white and covered in diamond dust glitter. When everyone walked outside to see the final windows, Elizabeth gasped. The horses glowed like crystals against the black velvet backdrop.

People fluttered out of their offices like moths drawn to streetlights.
"Who made these wonderful horses?" they asked. When the crew
pointed to Elizabeth, people showered her with praise: "Stunning!"
"Magical!" "Breathtaking!" Like her flying horses, Elizabeth was flying
high among the clouds.

The next day at the official *Wings of Wonder* unveiling, onlookers stood mesmerized by her trio of flying horses. They'd never seen anything like it! Shoppers overflowed into the street and blocked traffic, trying to get a glimpse of the mystical window displays. The windows even made national news!

The headlines caught the attention of many people. One admirer put Elizabeth in touch with the owners of a marine and animal park. They loved her work and invited her to be their artist-in-residence. At last, here was Elizabeth's chance to observe live exotic animals for as long as she liked. She imagined herself moving as if in their bodies: the stretch of a giraffe's neck . . . the crouch of a cheetah . . . the flap of an elephant's ears.

In her mind she traced their surface lines.

She went to work, recreating the beautiful creatures before her.
One animal sculpture at a time, Elizabeth built her own wire zoo.

Then one afternoon, while standing inside her life-sized sculpture of a bear, Elizabeth's skin tingled. She was suddenly looking through the bear's eyes. She felt it breathing and heard the drumming of its heartbeat. She and the bear's spirit were melded together as one.

In this moment Elizabeth realized that's what she'd been seeing all along! The animals' energy lines, their life forces. And now she had finally succeeded in sharing them with the world.

Ever since she was a baby, Elizabeth struggled to hold things in her right hand. When she was four years old, she watched her older sisters and brother make pretty pictures in coloring books and wanted to copy them. No one ever realized that Elizabeth was left-handed. She kept using her right hand because it was expected of her. Her struggle to find some way besides drawing to release her creativity led Elizabeth to keep trying new things and using creative problem-solving to evolve her own unique techniques for making wire sculptures.

Mr. Curran recommended art school to many of his graduating students, but not to Elizabeth. "You'd have a lousy time, kid. They'd think you were too fixated over the wire, and they'd want you to balance it out with all that other stuff that gave you so much grief," he told her. Elizabeth went to a junior college for one semester before getting married and starting a family. She made her little wire animals while raising a daughter and began selling her wire animals at craft fairs as a way to make some extra money. At first she worried people might not see her pieces as "real art." But some fairgoers told her she was a true wire sculptor. This boosted her confidence and encouraged her to stick with making art. When Elizabeth saw how much people loved her

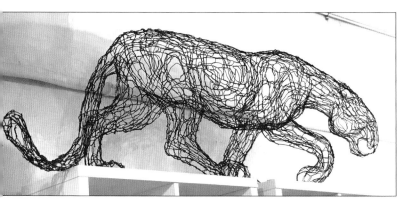

art, she got a hopeful inkling that being a wire sculptor might be her lifelong creative path. She went on to invent new wiring techniques, such as collapsible forms that can be reshaped after shipping.

In 2004 Elizabeth Berrien founded Wire Sculpture International, the worldwide guild of wire sculptors. Although the guild is not currently active, Elizabeth still goes by "Godmother of Wire," leading the contemporary wire sculpture movement. She continues to experiment and inspire other artists and students to think about wire and art in new, unique ways. More than fifty years after making her first sculpture, Elizabeth keeps enchanting people all over the world with her growing wire zoo. Her sculptures grace private collections, galleries, and public places worldwide.

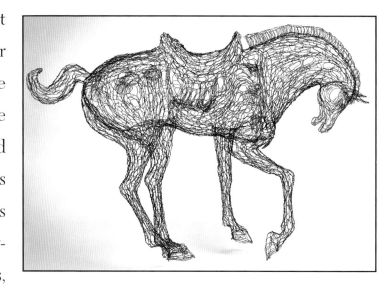

Elizabeth's studio

In Louisville, Kentucky, her Pegasus (flying horse with a wingspan of seventeen feet) has been hanging in the airport since 1985. It has become a beloved landmark. Each of her pieces—beautiful and flowing with energy—opens minds and eyes to see animals in a new way. To learn more and see a video of Elizabeth making wire art, go to www.wirezoo.com.

To my teacher and mentor Kenneth G. Curran,
who set me on a creative path that changed my life
—E. B.

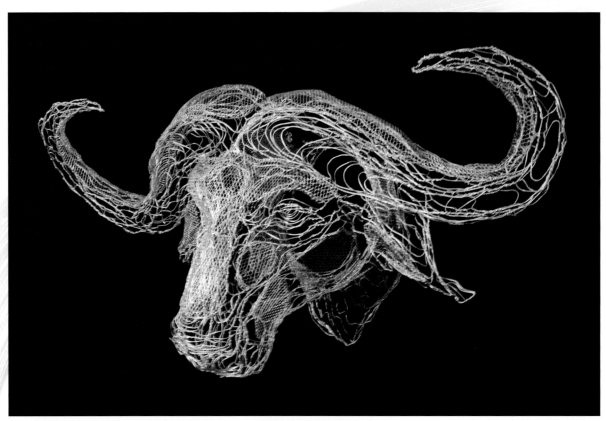